"Venus in Pisces"

Poems and Letters

by Kiara Blanchette

Copyright 2024 by Kiara Blanchette

All rights reserved.

No portion of this book may be reproduced in any form without written permission from the publisher or author, except as permitted by U.S. copyright law.

Title: Venus in Pisces
ISBN: 978-1-7383581-0-6

Printed and bound in the United States of America

Publisher: Kiara Blanchette-Ragoonanan

Cover Design by Kiara Blanchette
Cover Artwork: Ian Dagnall Computing/Alamy
Interior Collages by Lindsey Wagner

This book is dedicated to:

my younger self and my higher self.
may the three of us coexist and prosper.

Author's Note:

This book has been completely hand-typed by
myself on my trusty and beloved typewriter
that I've owned since I was 16. As such,
the pages of this book are not perfect.
Inside, you will find smudge marks, minor typos,
and portions where things have been crossed out
and typed over on washi tape. This book comes
from the most human and imperfect parts of me
and my hope is that these pages reflect that.
This is the closest one can get to reading
my diary. Love is messy and imperfect.
Just like this book.

Foreword

"Venus in Pisces" is about this inflation,
this obsession with infatuation. The desire to
sit and stew in it. To bathe in the way the words
pour out of you. The heat flush to the cheeks.
The ache in the heart long after.

This book is a curious documentation of whatever
romantic love has meant to me over the
past 7 years. I've arranged this collection
chronologically, organized by date written.

I've been writing this book since I was 19.
I've watched myself grow up on these pages.

These are my initial heart doodles. My notebook
scribbles. My moon date revelations. My crying
and softening. My hardening and resisting.
An analysis of the attachment I have to longing
and to sorrow.

It is deeply personal, but has poured out of me
in ways I've deemed too beautiful not to share.
I hope these reach you well.

Love endlessly,
Kiara

September 18th, 2017

Every day,
someone flies by
on the wrong side of the road.
The universe offers
no explanations.
Cites math.
Cites fate at the hands of
the eternally spinning wheel.
Pray it never stops.
I dream that all I am
capable of creating
is a life in which
we are full
and satisfied.

September 20th, 2017

"Passive You"

We are constantly creating in empty space.
I'm not good at math,
but this is all addition.
I fill any room with a body
half the size of yours
and words and words and words
that could secure themselves
around the Earth
like a belt
when put in sequence.
I worry about running out of space.
What it looks like when
the entire stadium is screaming
at once.
Oh, the irony.
Your passive to my aggresive,
silence has never been
this loud and clear.

September 20th, 2017

When was the last time I wrote in full sentences?
I'm always
eluding and alluding.
Writing around the thing
is such a dying art.
Coming close is
what you want.
It's what I can't give you,
or maybe so
in anything but perfection.
I can give it to you
in all that is
imperfection.

September 25th, 2017

We never cry over boys,
only we do...
and we hate ourselves for it.
I recognize that I am selfish,
but self-awareness is worth nothing
without action.
I keep my needs valid
in questionable conditions.
I do not beg.
I am
blatantly forward in my reverse psychology.
It is not your idea.
I need you to know that
I am red and buzzing.
A cry for help
is something else entirely
without tears.
The mocking tone
of a read receipt
reminds me that
someone new to text
and enough deep breaths
can prepare me
for movement all too much
away from you.
Take note.

October 4th, 2017

"B-Sides"

Dear M,

By now you know that I am always getting ahead of myself. I watch the tortoise trip the hare, and I am both of them. There are parts of me that move faster than others. My head faster than my heart and hands faster than my feet, but I find myself at ultimate distortion right in front of you.
I must apologize for my behavior as of late. I am a pixelated hologram of past, present, and future that hasn't yet figured out how to sit still as the needle skips across our broken record.
Times with you are poems b-sides. I need loss to write the way I imagine you leave because you know I'll always be there waiting when you get back.
I am nearsighted in both fore and hind. I keep my heart under lock and no key, or maybe one I lost and found in your back pocket.

The truth is, I trust with true conviction that I
am afraid of hurting you, and to a lesser degree
that I am scared of hurting myself. I need you to
know that I don't need gently. I fall deeper
every time I fear that I will lose you - this
happens like clockwork, fruit and color. I am
dynamite burning at both ends, but I won't tell
you fast enough for you to let me go.
I don't want you to let me go.

I've spent a good while steamed and spinning in
thoughts of loving you for a good time, not a
long one, but I toy with the idea of having both.
I never thought I wanted both. I fear oblivion
and falling so deeply into you that I lose
myself. I am trying to find a graceful way to
accept that I already have. And if it's true...
if it's true that I've found myself, at sea,
a lone anchor... would you sink with me?

December 27th, 2017

"Just Like Magic..."

Goodbye has always been a figure for you. Something I never really needed to come to terms with. I have yet to say anything for the last time, and to be honest, I'm far too young for a last time. The adventurous love dulls in my presence. I give flesh and pound and get static. The kind that makes your heart hurt. I quantify love by a noticeable negative. The way I only know I love you because of the way I hate without you. Take of that what you will. Distance is losing its effectiveness. In the sense that you can grow comfortable in any circumstance. Maybe so comfortable that with you seems foreign.
So comfortable, I re-introduce myself every time. A handshake for good business. Transactional. Calculating, and oddly linear. I've been told I'm good with words the way you're good at that disappearing act. The magic trick. And they all just want to know how you do it. How you got so good at pretending you don't care, that you didn't even notice when you stopped pretending.
Just like magic...

by another coat that was warmer and softer, but that I did not love. Why is it that we lose the things we love, and things cavalier cling to us and will be the measure of our worth after we're gone?

Then it occurred to me. Perhaps I absorbed my coat. I

January 2nd, 2018

I never get past the feeling that
I've met everyone.
Until I meet someone new...
and then I've met everyone.

April 26th, 2018

"Happy Fucking Birthday."

Seems Winter had us wrapped around his finger
like the tightest of pinky promises.
All straight jacket to routine
and no space for swaying.
Your old love is just
a hop, skip, and a jump away
from something less familiar.
A metered and calculated distance.
The house of a heart
you called home
is learning what an empty room feels like
and hates it.
If ever she had it in her
to be so poetic,
she would say,
"blank space is the writer's playground."
I'm just guessing.

July 11th, 2018

"Tearless"

I.

  She asks about me, the great big love
that broke you until her.
Finds me at palms open questioning.
"I think I just want to know."
And so do I.
Who finds you?
Post-spiral,
wide eyes and rhymes phonetically,
in a Georgian haze,
newfound independence strapped to your back.

II.

I stop writing and pick back up right
where I left off, desperate for understanding.
You don't fall out of love any faster
than you fell into it.
You only love differently.
The love I have for you now is tortured.
Lies on the premise that
if you fell to your knees now,
begging,
I'd have only enough in me
to take you at arm's length.
Just far enough for an echo.
And to hear me,
repeatedly at new odds.
At times, a sharp-noted pang of,
"love just doesn't look like this anymore."
It's lighter.
It passes through me,
tearless.

October 15th, 2018

"Melophobia"

And feel the chorus rush right through you...
This is music at its purest contemporary good.
When the poet gets past her own pretenses,
opens the floodgates.
What's that phobia?
The one some New Jersey's Melanie
is cradling.
I am already coming to terms
with the fact that
there will be a day you hate me,
or a day you see me in the street
and hope I don't see you back.
You can slip away gently.
I'm not ready.
Because our movie just started
and the opening credits are
your head between my thighs
and the end sequence is you
walking away for the last time,
and me taking your number
out of my phone.
Because I wrote another book.
Because you read this poem.
Because you warned me,
and once this pen gets to work,
I'm bound to you,
my story's new protagonist.

Because you didn't come here
for girls to write poetry about you,
you came to be achingly average
and kill time until you're ready to punch out.
Your starving artist generation
is only starving
for a love you won't let get too close.

(this is a poem I wrote on a bus
on the way to a job I hated.)

October 22nd, 2018

"An artistic exorcism."

And he would give you up in a heartbeat for
something sacrilegious. For drugs or love like one.
Wait. There's better simile out there, we know
this. Let's try that again.

You drop the cynicism, and become someone who loves
deeply and repeatedly like you've never been
hurt before. Like you're God's child and he loves
you like the rest of the blind.

This route is getting smoother. I wake up and
don't want to die, but I do want to stay in bed.
I get up. I'm proud of myself for that, is that
sick? Is it horrible that I give myself a trophy
for being alive? Still being alive.
For not killing myself years ago. Anyways.

Let's talk about not scaring people away.
How excited are you?
For new love and doors you can walk out of.
For so much money that it
stops existing in real life.
For boys you won't pay to hurt you.

October 31st, 2018

and who do I love?
someone invisible I haven't met yet
and let's dissect that,
shall we?

October 31st, 2018

So you want to live an artful life.
The thickness of you
split down the middle
to reveal you
in your purest pure poetry.

Inside,
your thousand man choir
is harmonizing all at once.
The rising.

Imagine never being alone.
I think alone is everything.

November 28th, 2018

"Poem Meet Poet"

Poem meet poet.
Poet wonders if she'll ever be able
to write poetry again.
Wonders if she can fall in love
so she can have something new to say.
Figures she can write a book
about the next person who breaks her heart.
Poet wonders
if the boy who doesn't answer
her text messages
might just be in love with her.
(spoiler alert: he's not.)
Wonders if
she places her hand
on the small of his back
and slides it upwards just slightly
to where she can feel his heart
beat through his ribcage,
figures she can pinpoint
the exact moment his heart
skips a beat.
Wonders if she can make a home for herself
right inside that empty space.

Says it only lasts a fraction of a second,
but she swears she can make herself
small enough to fit.
And that's what it is,
isn't it?
That love is just shapeshifting
and we're all dying
to be vessels
someone can
pour themselves into.

(this is a poem about realizing you need to stop checking to see if that one person watched your Instagram stories.)

March 23rd, 2019

"Happy Fucking Birthday Part II"

For one reason or another, I'm stuck in the same
pattern of being pulled by the neck.
Imagine putting a year's worth of days between
you and someone else, only to find yourself
right back where you started.
We're still chained to the sun and moon's
tide pulling dance, but you are not
the big love that takes the door off its hinges.

Time spent between you and the next person
to leave me reeling is almost the best dead air
I could ask for.

Sneaking into my corner of the internet is
a free show. You can stay to watch me fall apart
if you'd like.

April 12th, 2019

"Art for Art's Sake"

We're always standing at the foot of the goddess.
She places the pen in your hand. Take notes.
To which she professes ego is the death of the
artist. That the performative nature of all
of this is much too much to bear.
Is introduced to all of her art
as something separate from her.
Someone new she meets every time pen hits paper.
That in every iteration of it
is a new introduction.
Writer's block
is a lot like...
a lot like being buried.
Buried alive, I mean. The waiting.
The goddesses of creativity offer up
a new human sacrifice.
One to fuel good art and heartache.
The pen is in your hand
to make art for art's sake.

April 12th, 2019

"Mid-death, as she falls"

A scorned lover and the wife of an
ever-unfaithful man run a red light at the same
intersection and there isn't a sorry I can
conjure up that will ever make that ok
for either of us.

Men like him are indefinitely perturbed by the
cyclical nature of time. Wonder why in their
hands and as far enough as the eye can see
are the kinds of choices that leave
the cars up in flames
every
single
time.

June 25th, 2019

"Unmatched."

Somehow, fate is tearing you to shreds this week.
You are one or two bases
from things we can consider forgetting
and all of it is your fault.
Maybe it isn't all your fault,
but it sure does feel like it.
In real life,
you are somewhere waiting still
for bells to ring
or chimes to chime,
and they are out in the rush
keeping new numbers straight.
Phoning friends.
You're always either
finding yourself in tight spaces
or just are one.
The days are rushing at and past you faster
than the crash of any wave
you've ever found yourself under.
You are endlessly palms down in mercy.
In a sense, you've done the best you know.
In a sense, that is all you have
to give.

yet he sees. He recognizes voices within silence, history within negative space. He conjures ancestors who are not ancestors, with such precision that the gilded threads of an embroid

October 19th, 2019

Dear J,

Words are somehow harder to get out when your heart isn't busy breaking, but I've been told the easiest thing to write is the truth. When the ability to trust myself eludes me, my ability to trust you is second nature. I throw away my mirrors and replace them with your eyes, your hand starts exactly where mine ends. The curve of my side fits right into the front of yours. Blindfolded, my skin and your skin are no different. If this were a love letter, I would tell you that we are pieces of a jigsaw puzzle made complete together. If this were a love letter, I would say that with you, time escapes me tenfold. I blink and all eternity slips through my fingers. To admit that time existed for me before you, I mean, to admit that time existed for you before me seems unconscionable. I retrace my steps and place myself in an alternate universe where we run in infinite concentric circles that never meet. I retrace my steps and pinpoint the exact moment things fell apart so that we could fall together. I imagine the cosmic mathematicians somewhere up there, carrying the one that leads me right to your front door. The truth is, we are no coincidence, but coincidentally, I am yours.

April 29th, 2021

"Cusp."

I'm 23. I know better now. I once walked face first into a plate glass door with my chin right forward. I stopped writing because I fell in love. I stopped writing because I didn't want to create a world other than the one I was living in. I have space for more worlds now. New worlds. A full moon ray casted through rose quartz crystal light. This moment feels like it could burst open, like it's ripping at the seams. The tension of the fabric around my back, swelling and thinning each thread to the micro unit of its last breath. I'm not a size 2 anymore. Exhale. I soften in places and harden in others. I asked a stranger to teach me how to trust. Every day, I let go of a small piece of control. I let go of a small piece of the illusion of control. I let the Earth catch me every time. Someone told me that's called grounding. I walk somewhere on the line, knowing home is here and there both at once. I know enough to know I'm crazy and also enough to know that crazy people don't know they're crazy. So I sit here on the cusp.

November 17th, 2022

"Boundaries"

What a burden
to be stuck with this
puppy dog baby girl.
She'll probably never leave you alone.
She might fall in love with you
if you give her enough attention.
She may have
fallen in love already.
Tell her
 you can only see her every 2 weeks.
Tell her you need to slow things down to
30km an hour. Tell her
that we're driving in a school zone.
That kids could get hurt.
Tell her
speed bump, speed bump, speed bump.
Tell her you can't handle
her hands on your face.
Tell her not to look at you like that.
She knows exactly which way.
That way.
Like she wants you to crawl inside her
and find a space to get comfortable.
Like she wants you to make a little dog bed
out of her heart.

Tell her to stop crawling on her knees for you.
But you don't want her to stop.
Tell her you can't watch.
Tell her you can watch,
but with one eye closed.
Tell her she's perfect,
but not too perfect.
Tell her she's just fun for now.
Tell her you're both on the same page.
Tell sweet, sweet baby girl
she can fall apart in your arms.
Tell her the boy is no good.
Tell her you want every inch of her
in your mouth,
but tell her that you'll spit her out.
Tell her you can't be the one
to pick up the pieces
when you break her,
when you SHATTER her.
Tell her
you saw this coming.

November 21st, 2022

"Ethical Non-Monogamy"

How am I
supposed to go on a date
    with someone else
   and think about
anything but
    kissing you.
Kissing you and kissing you.
Flour on my face,
hands on my ass,
    kissing you.
Missing him and kissing you.
Missing you and missing you.
    Mouth on my neck,
kissing you.
    Little love bites
kissing you.
Pushing me away,
kissing me anyway.
Kissing you.

December 9th, 2022

"Stranger and strangest yet"

So I kissed someone else just to have another taste on my tongue. She kissed nothing like you. Felt nothing like you. Nothing like knowing you. She felt like stranger and strangest yet. She was neither soft nor squishy. I held her all in one go. My arms around her waist with too much space to spare. She pushed me up against a tree and there was too much wood. Too much cold.
(I wish you'd stop being stubborn.)
I wish you'd get over yourself and realize we don't just rush our faces toward each other like this. Like the world is burning. Like we'll die if we don't. That's not normal. To drip like that. To beg like that. You forget the way you never get over your first. The way you opened a door that's been locked for god knows how long. The way everything piling up had been pressed up behind it just waiting to spill out. And it oozed. Exploded, actually, like a flame to a glass balloon.
You and I have been anything but inconsequential. You pulled the door right off its hinges.

December 11th, 2022

"horizontal and perpendicular"

There are pieces of you that still feel stuck inside me. A phantom itch from your finger there and a spot on my back you never touched. A spot on my back that aches for your touch. And each thing I want to say to you but can't lingers inside of me begging to come out. I think about texting you and don't. I think about sending you a song and do. You don't answer. I maybe regret sending it, but I don't regret thinking about you when I listen to it and wanting you to think of me when you listen to it too. That story I want to tell you. How my date went last night. How I've wished every time on every date that it were you sitting across from me instead.
That time you were in my bed.
Horizontal and perpendicular.

The way being face down screaming into my pillow is just one of the voice notes I have to keep myself from sending. Listening to your voice notes and having them echo like something playing over itself 10 times at once. (because I've heard them so many times.) Because I shamefully hold you like my little not so secret secret. Because I swore we were the team you forgot about. Because you don't know whether you're coming or going, and lately you've only been going.

December 16th, 2022

"i miss winters in westchester"

I pour back into myself, dive head first into books. 100 The Cut article tabs open. I bookmark all of them. I read none of them.

I fill my own cup till it overflows. He sends soup to my door and I feel so guilty. He hasn't been the only one to feed me lately. I leave the chocolates in the advent calendar so I have something to look forward to. The girls at my neighborhood pub know me by name now.
"Tequila Sunrise?" I've always wanted to be a regular.

I hand my number out on little ripped up sheets of lined paper. I await texts from 3 girls I know I won't be hearing from. They are each both too close and too far for comfort.

A tall medicated man who should continue going to therapy grabs my head in his hands and tells me he just wants to massage my brain for hours. Tells me I'm the first thing to give him hope since the breakup. Tells me he loves me. He sends me SoundCloud links and I don't answer. He says "I see you." and I don't answer. He makes me a 20-track playlist and I tell him he probably shouldn't.

The petite Irish blonde who kisses with the remnants of cigarette smoke still on her mouth texts me and I feel nothing. I think about someone else's mouth. How much more substantial it felt to hold her. How she kissed my neck and I actually liked it. How she left bruises on my thighs that I pressed my fingers to for days and days later.

What's that sound? The sound of so much self-searching. Searching for someone who is honey to the knives in my throat.
Pure syrup sweetness.

December 24th, 2022

"Four Out of Five"

I write things down
so I don't forget them.
I was introduced to some of
my favorite songs
by people I don't speak to anymore.
None of your recommendations
have made the list,
but I still manage
to make every song I listen to
about you.
I try and nail down
the way you can keep
your hands around my neck
while at a distance.
Why I'm determined to keep them there.
How the indentations
from your rings
can still be perceived
to this day.

December 26th, 2022

"Urgency"

There's always
 a learning curve
 when you first
 kiss someone new
The degree
 of head tilt needed.
The give and the take.
More give, less take.
 More take.
 More take.
 More take.

December 28th, 2022

"Finally, one that rhymes."

Time spent waiting for people to be fair
will prove to be unfruitful.
Time spent waiting for people to care
will leave you sitting in despair,
She wouldn't dare.
Not after playing with your hair,
not after that kiss on the stairs,
the way she stares, the way she glares.
She swears she was aware, she declared
she would never leave you beyond repair.
They told you to beware,
but you couldn't prepare,
the way she ate your heart,
and left not a bite to spare.
Now they can't compare.
Everything you bared, everything you shared,
it's all in the air.
Your scent all over those sweaters she wears,
It was just an affair.
Laissez-faire. Laissez-faire.
She was never yours to begin with,
she has always been theirs.

January 2nd, 2023

"Two Halves of a Crime"

She smiles like
she's getting away with something.
My heart in her hands,
I don't even notice.
I always wondered why it felt
like we were co-conspirators.
Two halves of a crime.
She whispers how she wishes
I could sleep in her bed tonight.
I raise my finger to her lips.
Shh.
Don't say that.

January 5th, 2023

I'm getting better at just
putting on my pants
and going to the store
at the first thought of it.

Less hem, less haw.

We're out of milk.
Boots on. Fists up.

January 8th, 2023

"The Three Graces"

and back to the bites on the thighs...
young and eager to please,
i drip off her lips
with the levity you're dying for.
her tattoos, melted on wet black ink,
butter and silk are a close second.
i fuck someone who shares a name with
my favorite therapist.
close enough.

January 8th, 2023

"The Herald's Postman"

You are drowning in nonchalance now,
almost numb, almost sedated.
The air between your words is sticky
like cough syrup. I wonder
if you feel anything at all.
If it turns out you've
locked all your thoughts away for safekeeping,
let me know if you lost the key.
I'd like to have a word
with something you left in the box.
Tell me you poked holes in it.
I wave my hand in front of your eyes
to find no one home for good.
Your mailbox overflowing.
Weeks old newspapers
spilling onto the front lawn.
How naive of me,
I thought you'd leave a light on.

January 14th, 2023

"crunch"

Every night,
I go out and I wait
for something interesting to happen.
For experience to fall into my lap.
I beg for a little more life to crunch on.
The meat of it between
my molars.
I miss you,
but slightly less
when my mouth is full.
I chew slowly.

January 15th, 2023

"First"

How does it feel
to be the yardstick
with which I measure
every girl
that comes after you?
To be the blueprint.
I unfold a large sheet of paper
etched with pen scribbles
and hold it up to their faces,
scrunching my nose
as I compare and contrast.
Softer please. Tougher please.
Bigger please.

January 23rd, 2023

I came back for one last hug.
A swingy hug. A twisty hug.
One where your head
is tucked into my neck,
the base of your chin
pressed into my shoulder.
Where your hand reaches around
and you rub my back gently.
There there baby girl.
I missed you too.

January 23rd, 2023

It's funny because when I start writing,
it's usually because someone's given me
an indication of not thinking about me
or about us at all.
And that's when I pick up my pen.
To fill that empty space.
I don't write poetry
when I'm being thought about.
It's my way of letting things exist
in some world.

January 24th, 2023

"Growing Pains"

For some reason, you exist
in the same cinematic universe
as my cousin.
Don't know how to explain that one.
I will miss you for a while,
but apparently they call
this feeling in my bones
"growing pains".
Stop pulling at my leg.
Now you've run off with it.
I want it back.
Pains and all.
Sew me up, no anesthetic.
Lick the wound.
Touch your finger
to the scar.
Feel the raised lines?
The way that spot
will never be perfect again?
It's evidence
you were here.

March 14th, 2023

"The Perfect Bite"

I'll go back to the lamb,
until shedding season,
at least.
Until there is less
of it in my mouth.
I spend too much time
chewing on reason.
      Dare I say,
reason went out the door
      when you touched
the tip of your tongue to it.
Steam rising off the bite.
The way mothers test hot milk
on the underbelly of the wrist;
they'll scald
the softest parts of themselves
to protect the other.
      (some acts
           are a synonym for care.)

May 17th, 2023

"Glutton for Punishment"

Dear A,

It's been easier for me to write about you than to write to you, but courage tells me that's just because I don't think you want to hear what I have to say.

I've been hiding from you, scared that if you saw all of me and rejected me still, there'd be no safe place to duck for cover for miles and miles.

I lied in my voice note. There was no innocence in my checking up on you. I'm as calculating now as the day we first locked eyes in the front room. I knew I wanted you then, and knew somehow I'd have you. I haven't let go of the knowing somehow I'll have you, despite every voice inside of me and out telling me to let it go. I cannot let it go.
I'm sorry for the inconvenience.

More time has passed than maybe it was even worth
to you, and maybe you've forgotten all about it,
but I haven't. Time for me is marked precisely,
before and after. I haven't been the same since.

To act as though you haven't occupied more of
my brain space than I care to admit means to
lie more than I'd like to.

Everything you didn't want to happen had already
happened by the time I knew your name, it was
too late. I wanted you to ruin me.

I know the last thing you wanted was to wreck me.
You did everything you could to stop it. I did
everything I could to be pummeled by the weight
of it. I wanted to be crushed by something bigger
than me.

Am I wrong in thinking you wanted me more than
you knew what to do with? Tell me I'm wrong
and I'll go away for good.

I've been in and out of flings for months now,
searching for an ounce of that knotted twisted
feeling in my stomach. I want to feel sick.
I haven't felt sick since the last time you
looked at me and ironically, that feels like
something I need to get checked out.

I'm embarrassed to tell you how many poems I've
written about a blip in time I've blown up to be
large enough so I can exist inside it.
That I've thought of every single way I want you
to .... I'll spare you the details. How every
girl that came after you was a desperate attempt
at finding that feeling again.

I'm smart enough to know that you don't deserve
any of this, but against my better judgment,
I'm a glutton for punishment.

When i say i wanted consideration
i think what i wanted was to
be seen by you for what i was.
at times i felt like you did see me,
but if you really did then nothing
else would matter, i reckon. i wouldn't
be here writing you a letter wrong
~~you wanted me~~ am i ~~get~~ in
thinking you wanted me more than
you knew what to do with?
~~[scribbled out]~~ Tell me i'm
wrong and i'll go away for go~~[od]~~

that i've managed to walk away from everyone else with my heart intact, you knocked the wind out of me like a sucker punch that came so fast, I had no time to brace for impact.

if i'm being honest, id let you hit me again. against my better judgement, i'm a glutton for punishment

May 18th, 2023

They say this city's small,
but I haven't found you
in it yet.
Not for lack of trying.
I pressed my face to the glass
window of that bar
you told me you went to
that one time;
you probably haven't
been back there since,
but I haven't stopped thinking
of it as yours
since the day you mentioned it.

July 19th, 2023

If I didn't know any better, I could think
I love you. I do know better though.
I watch the hour hand hit our time
repeatedly.
You are hooked onto a thread that
tugs at my deepest gut senses.

you say "romantic" and I say "upset",
you say "delicious" and I say,
it should have been me.
if you could have anyone by your side,
why wouldn't it be me?

if you're entangled and I text you, does
the web just get bigger or do you cut me
out of it? I am so far from you now and yet
sex with me should just be sex with you,
and her and her and her should just be you.
we could make the web smaller, start a new
one, tear it down...
reintroduce ourselves.

who are you now?
you would love me now,
you would love me
now I swear.

I'm somehow waiting here still to be considered.
For us to bridge the gap between once was
and still to come. For me, still, to come.

She is like you in many ways,
mainly in the way she asserts herself.
Yes and no, this not that, touch me not,
fold for you, close back up,
and carry on.

In the want for little and yet get everything
and still want more, want less from someone else,
want space. To want or not to want, that
is the question.

        pull me back into your orbit.
pull me into your
                wet hot
    tornado fire
                    thunder hurricane
  natural disasters you make with your hands

  the things you touch,
            let me crumble
                  with them.

July 28th, 2023

(red to blue to purple to yellow)

so I will sit at this desk and write
until there is none of you
left in me,
until you are expelled, until I forget
how to spell
your name
is carved into my memory,
my headboard,
marked into my thighs
with your teeth
how could I forget
how could I forget
we were soaked,
soaking,
rain pounding off the hood.
there is still, somehow,
too much of you to hold onto.
I grip the air,
remember a fistful of your neck,
a mouthful of skin,
soft flesh, and enough of it,
to carry me
to the next love,
and so on.

I walked across the park.
A girl pulled her jeans off slowly.

*

Once, making love with a girl,
I thought I was someone else.

August 26th, 2023

Ready for the soundtrack
to the new season.
The pedal steel resonance.
The chill at the bow of the boat,
the awakening.
The once was hot,
but now am not.
The fresh air denim skirt warrior march.
The crisp browns and bronzes.
Red lipstick delicious green apple
more yogurt, more waffles.
More syrup, yes syrup.
More warmth and
that time of year we write about.
I want passion in a turtleneck.
Tights you rip. Boots made to walk in.

September 26th, 2023

You can't come back from knowledge.
Trust me,
 I've tried to rebirth myself
into ignorance, back to a world
I could trust you.
God stopped me at a red light
and told me the only way out is through.
Told me knowing begets knowing.
That we are learning far too much too quickly.
That consciousness has evolved to know
until it consumes itself.
The stars watch you, and they know everything.
That's why they burn off
one by one.

September 30th, 2023

"Happy Medium"

New York is underwater.
I wish that was a metaphor for something.
I wish there was one less body of water
between us, two less islands, and an
unflinching sense of knowing.

I think about how many things get lost
in the Hudson River.
How many cell phones, how many bodies.
How if you cross two bridges to see me,
how many times do you think of me in an hour?
You don't have to answer that.

If you pull at one more string,
I'll unravel until I'm just a pile of thread
you can sew me back together with.

There is not much worth breaking for anymore.
At least so I thought.

I patch myself up
for the 9th time,
only to find
my heart is still
a blinking red sign
that reads,
"WELCOME."

October 6th, 2023

"not unless polyamory"

I reach for a hand to hold for no reason.
just because hands,
just because comfort,
just because protection.

I think one day,
there will be one hand,
and I won't think about another
until my index finger fills its whole palm,
gripping me with the kind of love that
can only come from
being made by someone.

and I want to make someone.
I want to know why we can't.
I want to know why holding me
by the neck an arm's length away
and looking into my eyes just means
two heartbeats and never three.

not unless polyamory,
not unless a stranger gets to merge himself
with me and my purity,
but I want us and our purity.
soft hands, light eyes, a woman's touch.
a baby that looks just like us.

a daughter with your last name and my nose,
your eyes, our heart.
one that comes from us fitting into each other
in a way no man ever could.

I reach for a hand to hold for that reason.

because legacy,
because lineage.
because love that multiplies
down a twisted chain we pass on and on.

I walk away, empty handed as all ever.

Like two round pegs with only square holes to fit
into, we slip through each other repeatedly,
never really gripping enough to stick.

Full of nothing that can latch onto the womb.

Loving never enough to give birth.

October 17th, 2023

"daydreaming angels nearing intimacy"

And tell me why I think about the girl, her hand to my back, chest to my face. Pressed against her car or hands touching on bar, I wonder if I would enjoy calling her my girlfriend more than I would taking care of her when she's sick.

She handles me like she'd handle an aristocrat's daughter. With dominion. Like my hands too delicate to touch doors, my spine needing to be traced to be kept upright. There is value in the things left unsaid, but less so than the ones expressed.

I breathe deeply holding a "je t'aime" in my throat. She grabs it firmly, but struggles with making eye contact. Struggles with saying my name when she's not disappointed. I let her fall asleep on me, her eyes closing around a message she'll respond to in the morning. One night, we sat face to face for hours, unblinking, playing with each others' hair until the sun came up. I haven't yet figured out which I prefer.

In 9 days, I'll run to her, some flaccid jump into a hand on my ass; legs wrapped around her torso like I missed her or something. Like I want to keep her upper half here with me. Then I wonder if distance is the invisible thread that pulls us each closer. A lasso circling my waist tugging me back to a space our faces can meet.

November 16th, 2023

"something better."

I did arts & crafts with my inner child
and she told me
she wants to be me when she grows up.
Said I look just like she imagined,
only prettier.
I hold her hand somewhere in mine,
and remember it used to hold my father's.
I am hardened,
but my hands stayed soft and small,
like he wanted to keep a part of me
he could recognize.
Someone told me
she is me still and will be forever,
but I know that I am something else now,
something better.

November 26th, 2023

"cross and continue crossing."

I will say I'm ready and
cry at least once weekly
and mean it every single time.
I cross and continue crossing.
I break and keep opening.
I shed and bleed and squirt
until the water runs clear.
I heal repeatedly
while the skin polishes itself
burning glistening
fiery perfect.
I am more ready now
than I was 3 months ago,
but I step into myself every day
like a suit I'm trying on for size,
like one that
still needs to be tailored.
I feel the extra fabric buckling
around my hips and waistline.
The pants sagging with each step.
The shoes
too big to walk in.

December 9th, 2023

"Long Distance, Low Maintenance"

I don't know how to explain
that her needs are my needs.
That she wants for what
I beg to give her.
I watch the sun melt
into the space behind the ocean
and think in there
is a pocket she could float in.
One I'd carve for her.
I write her poems instead.
Inky hands thumbing through
innumerable versions of I miss you
in this language or the other.
Watch my fingernails tap out lines
long enough to reach across the border.
They cut Vermont straight down the middle,
loop through Connecticut,
pass Yonkers and hook along the shore.
And there is more and more and more.
I open up my mind
and heart for the altering.
I have not much to give,
but attempts at peace,
and peace offerings.

January 13th, 2024

"Lust plus"

Another day where I
try not to say "I love you"
over text,
reach for every truthful alternative to
varying degrees of satisfaction.
"I adore you",
"I miss you",
"I want your hands on my face
or in my mouth or in my --",
back to the drawing board.
What a sweet thing you are.
I bet the best girls
make poems out of you,
bet the prettiest ones
doodle your name in their notebooks
with hearts for the i,
and my hearts for eyes see nothing else.

Just that word we don't say,
just looking for excuses
to buy you gifts or
book a flight just to kiss you,
just, just, just,
and must must must be love
because good god
I could not learn
to trust like this without it.
And I do love you,
no doubt about it.

January 29th, 2024

Because you think that it can't get hotter
than boiling, what can vaporize water at the
instant? Turn the body to dust for the mantle.
I decided to stop asking how it could get worse.
My saturn return begs me to hold on tight to
which vestige of my personality can put up
a fight, be either immovable or mutable in the
face of chaos. Roll over when necessary,
play dead when imperative, be a solid block
to take punches or blowbacks from the chopping,
lacerations to my thighs, be loud, but also
know when to shut up.
I think life is testing me now,
I open my palms up for the whipping,
say thank you and wipe the wine from my
mouth.

June 3rd, 2024

This is a poem for the girl born
with a heart too big for her body.
Crybaby, soft lover,
miss Venus in Pisces incarnate.
Who muses and communes with the moon,
has a direct line to Heaven,
and God always picks up.
Counts the stretch marks on her thighs
like every chance she's given, for every lie.
If only she weren't a lesson,
not a paragraph to underline,
she is tired of being the girl you lose
so you can learn to do better
next time.

www.ingramcontent.com/pod-product-compliance
Lightning Source LLC
Chambersburg PA
CBHW061750070526
44585CB00025B/2854